Where *is* Jesus?

Marjory Francis and Helen Gale

D1346283

Where is Jesus?

Where is Jesus?

Where is Jesus?

Eating supper.

Where is Jesus?

Washing feet.

Where is Jesus?

In the garden.

Where is Jesus?

Where is Jesus?

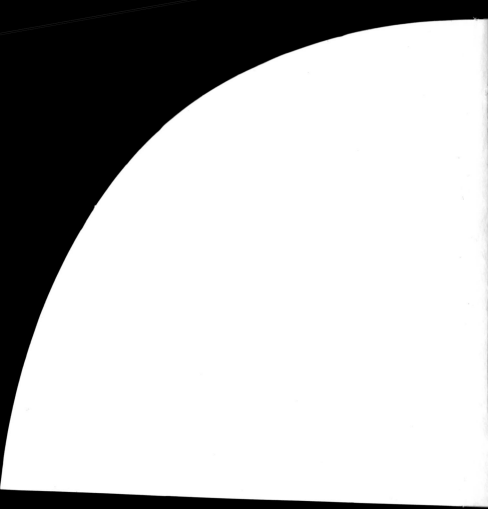

In a tomb.

Where is Jesus?

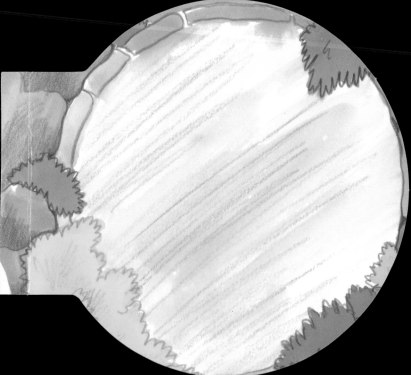

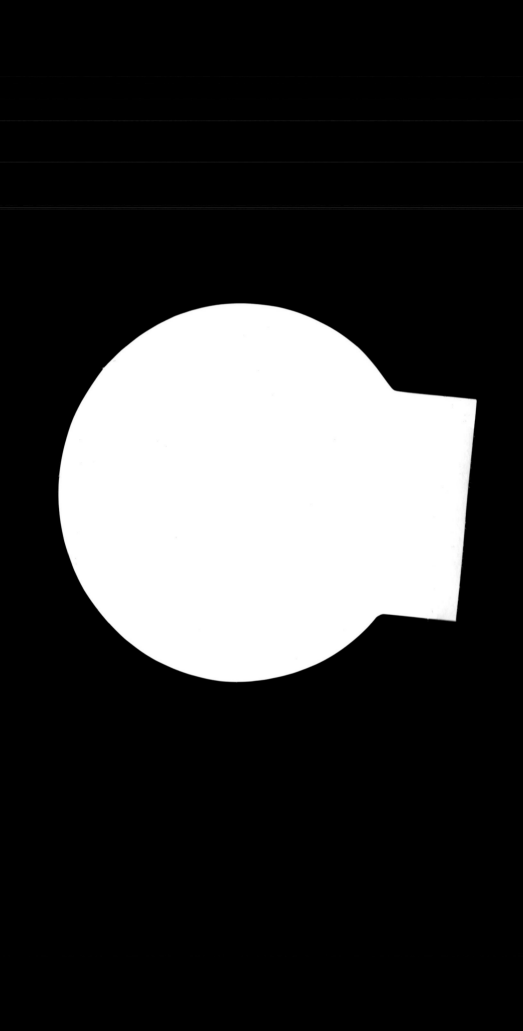

Where is Jesus?

Jesus did die on the cross, and he did come alive again! Now he is alive forever in heaven, loving us and watching over us.

Why don't you shout "hooray! Jesus is alive today!"?